MW01125654

Brigid and the Butter

A Legend about Saint Brigid of Ireland

Retold by Pamela Love
Illustrated by Apryl Stott

Pauline
BOOKS & MEDIA
Boston

Library of Congress Cataloging-in-Publication Data

Names: Love, Pamela, 1966- author. | Stott, Apryl, illustrator. Title: Brigid and the butter : a legend about Saint Brigid of Ireland / retold by Pamela Love ; illustrated by Apryl Stott.

Description: Boston, Mass. : Pauline Books & Media 2017.

Identifiers: LCCN 2016021514| ISBN 9780819812339 (hc.) | ISBN 0819812331 (hc.)

Subjects: LCSH: Brigid, of Ireland, Saint, approximately 453-approximately 524--Juvenile literature. | Brigid, of Ireland, Saint, approximately 453-approximately 524--Legends.

Classification: LCC BR1720.B74 L68 2017 | DDC 270.2092--dc23

LC record available at https://lccn.loc.gov/2016021514

Design by Mary Joseph Peterson, FSP
Illustrated by Apryl Stott

Published by Pauline Books & Media, 50 Saint Paul's Avenue, Boston, MA 02130–3491

Printed in the U.S.A.

BTB VSAUSAPEOILL8-2910065 1233-1

www.pauline.org
Pauline Books & Media is the publishing house of the Daughters of St. Paul, an international congregation of women religious serving the Church with the communications media.

1 2 3 4 5 6 7 8 9   21 20 19 18 17

For all those
who feed the hungry

Long ago in deep-green Ireland lived a bright-eyed slave girl named Brigid. She and her mother worked very hard for their master. By her tenth summer, Brigid was cooking, cleaning, and caring for the master's cows. Every day she led them to the meadow to graze and to drink from the stream there. Mornings and evenings she milked them. Besides all that, twice a week she spent hours making fresh butter.

Butter making was no easy job. Brigid poured the cream—the richest, thickest part of the milk—into a churn nearly as high as her chin. Into it went a thick paddle called a dash. Up and down, up and down, and on and on she dipped the heavy dash. Finally, when her aching arms could hardly go on, butter would appear, floating in the churn.

Next Brigid washed the butter in cold water
several times and salted it. Only then could she and
her mother enjoy the treat. Tired as she was, the
taste of freshly-buttered bread made all Brigid's work
worthwhile.

Yet Brigid's life wasn't all churning and chores. She liked walking on buttercup-covered fields and talking to the people in her village. She even got to see Bishop Patrick from time to time as he traveled throughout the countryside.

One warm afternoon, Brigid and her mother came upon a small group of people gathered around the bishop. "Once there was a huge crowd listening to Jesus," Bishop Patrick said. "He had been teaching them all day long. The people were really hungry and they had no food."

Oh no! Brigid thought. *It's terrible to be so hungry.*

"Jesus didn't want to send them away unfed," Bishop Patrick continued. "Then a boy in the crowd gave one of the disciples all the food he had brought with him—five small barley loaves and two fish." Moving to the front of the crowd Brigid heard the bishop say, "Do you know what happened next? Jesus blessed the food the boy had given up and everyone ate until they were full."

Brigid often thought about the gospel story Bishop
Patrick told them and the generous boy who gave all
the food he had. *Nobody asked the boy to give up his food;
he just did it anyway. And Jesus fed thousands of people with
only a little bread and two fish! I wish I could be like that
boy.*

One day, while her mother was away, Brigid did her usual chores. When she finished making the butter, she put it on a little dish and placed it on their bare table. It was the only food they had. It would be such a small supper if Mother couldn't bring bread back. Brigid sighed. *What if all we have to eat tonight is this butter?*

Just then Brigid heard a soft knock on the cottage door. Opening it she saw an old woman, almost as short as Brigid herself, but even thinner.

"Good day," the old lady said. "I wonder if you might help me. I've been walking all day long without a bite to eat. Do you have something you can spare?"

She felt sorry for the old lady, but Brigid didn't know what to do. She and her mother had eaten nothing that morning. What could she offer the hungry woman?

"Won't you come in and have a seat?" Brigid asked. "Mother will be home by sunset. She may bring home some food. We would be happy to share our supper with you."

The old woman shook her head. "Such a kind thought, but I can't wait. Do you have anything I can take now?"

"Nay, for we have nothing ourselves, or almost nothing." Turning, Brigid pointed to the small dish with its ball of butter on the otherwise bare table. "We've only this butter, with nothing to spread it on."

The woman's eyes turned misty with tears. "Butter . . . I can't remember the last time I had some. I hardly remember what it tastes like."

Brigid didn't know what to say. She could well believe that the thin old woman didn't remember the taste of butter. She looked as though she hardly ever got any food to eat. But Brigid also loved the taste of butter. She almost said, "I'm sorry." She almost shut the door. But she didn't.

She remembered Bishop Patrick's story. Brigid glanced at the churn standing in the corner. Making butter was a lot of work. Now she understood that helping others could be just as difficult. *Jesus, only you can feed thousands*, Brigid thought, *but I can give what I have to feed the one person before me.*

With skirt swirling Brigid spun around to pick up the butter. Holding it out, she said, "I pray you find someone who can give you bread to go with this. God be with you on your journey, ma'am."

The old woman's face brightened as she tucked the butter, dish and all, into her sack. "Thank you, my dear! May God repay you for your generosity!" With a smile, the old lady headed down the path.

Brigid's freckled nose wrinkled as she wondered
what her mother would say. But she didn't regret her
choice, even if it meant going to bed hungry.

"Lord, I'm glad that woman will have something
to eat," Brigid prayed. "But now my mother and I have
nothing. In your mercy, please provide for us, too."

With a sigh, she turned around . . . and saw *two* large dishes on the table, each piled high with butter she had not made!

Through her tears, Brigid prayed, "Thank you, Lord, for giving us so much butter, and also for the chance to give what I had before. Amen."

About
Saint Brigid

Saint Brigid was born around the year 453 in Ireland to her slave mother, Brocca, and pagan chieftain father, Dubhthach. Not too much is known about Brigid's early life, but tradition says that she and her mother knew Saint Patrick and that he may have baptized them.

Brigid's generosity, which we read about in this story, continued. In fact, it is said that her father was angry because Brigid often gave away food and her father's possessions. He went to the King of Ireland to complain about his daughter and to sell her. The king, however, recognized her goodness and ordered that Brigid be freed.

When she grew up, Brigid did not want to marry like other young women her age. She wanted to belong to God as a nun. Her father agreed in time, and he even gave her money with which to start the first of her many monasteries—places where people could live, work, and worship God. She was the leader (abbess) of a monastery in Kildare, which became a center of faith and learning. It was there that Brigid started an art school, where people learned metal work and how to illustrate Scripture with beautiful pictures.

There are many stories about Saint Brigid. One tells of how she was called to the bedside of a dying chieftain. As she sat beside him she told him about Jesus and wove a cross from the rushes on the floor. This is the origin of the famous Saint Brigid's cross. Wherever Brigid stayed, she made sure the poor and the sick were fed and cared for. Many people reported receiving miracles after Brigid prayed for them.

Saint Brigid is a patron saint of Ireland, dairymaids, midwives, and newborn babies. Her feast day is February 1, and she is Ireland's most famous female saint.

Prayer to
Saint Brigid

Saint Brigid, you gave food to someone who was hungry although your stomach was also empty. I want to be generous, too. Pray for me so that, like you, I may do what I can to help others. Help me to care for people in need, even when it isn't easy. Amen.

Pamela Love

After growing up in New Jersey, Pamela Love attended Bucknell University. She worked as a teacher and in marketing before turning to writing. She's the author of numerous picture books and has written many stories and poems in children's magazines. Pamela is also a contributor to *Family Matters: Thirteen Short Stories*, published by Pauline Books & Media. She lives with her husband and son in Maryland.

Apryl Stott

Apryl Stott loves to draw and paint. She studied illustration and design at Brigham Young University. Now, Apryl lives with her husband, two daughters, and six pet chickens in northern Nevada where she works as a freelance illustrator. Apryl has drawn pictures for books, card games, postcards, stickers, posters, school books, and lots of magazines. This is her third book for Pauline Books & Media. You can find out more about her work at aprylstottdesign.com.

Tales and Legends from

Who are the Daughters of St. Paul?

We are Catholic sisters. Our mission is to be like Saint Paul and tell everyone about Jesus! There are so many ways for people to communicate with each other. We want to use all of them so everyone will know how much God loves us. We do this by printing books (you're holding one!), making radio shows, singing, helping people at our bookstores, using the internet, and in many other ways.

VISIT OUR WEB SITE AT WWW.PAULINE.ORG

BOOKS & MEDIA

The Daughters of St. Paul operate book and media centers at the following addresses. Visit, call, or write the one nearest you today, or find us at www.paulinestore.org.

CALIFORNIA
3908 Sepulveda Blvd, Culver City, CA 90230 — 310-397-8676
3250 Middlefield Road, Menlo Park, CA 94025 — 650-369-4230

FLORIDA
145 S.W. 107th Avenue, Miami, FL 33174 — 305-559-6715

HAWAII
1143 Bishop Street, Honolulu, HI 96813 — 808-521-2731

ILLINOIS
172 North Michigan Avenue, Chicago, IL 60601 — 312-346-4228

LOUISIANA
4403 Veterans Memorial Blvd, Metairie, LA 70006 — 504-887-7631

MASSACHUSETTS
885 Providence Hwy, Dedham, MA 02026 — 781-326-5385

MISSOURI
9804 Watson Road, St. Louis, MO 63126 — 314-965-3512

NEW YORK
64 W. 38th Street, New York, NY 10018 — 212-754-1110

SOUTH CAROLINA
243 King Street, Charleston, SC 29401 — 843-577-0175

TEXAS
Currently no book center; for parish exhibits or outreach evangelization, contact:
210-569-0500, or SanAntonio@paulinemedia.com, or
P.O. Box 761416, San Antonio, TX 78245

VIRGINIA
1025 King Street, Alexandria, VA 22314 — 703-549-3806

CANADA
3022 Dufferin Street, Toronto, ON M6B 3T5 — 416-781-9131

¡También somos su fuente para libros,
videos y música en español!

SMILE
God loves you